WHAT WERE YOU THINKING?

Julian Stannard taught for many years at the University of Genoa and is now a Reader in Creative Writing at the University of Winchester. Previous poetry collections include *Rina's War* (Peterloo, 2001), *The Red Zone* (Peterloo, 2007) and *The Parrots of Villa Gruber Discover Lapis Lazuli* (Salmon, 2011). Critical work includes books on Fleur Adcock and Basil Bunting. He co-edited (with André Naffis-Sahely) *The Palm Beach Effect: Reflections on Michael Hofmann* (CB editions, 2013). His film poem 'Sottoripa', in collaboration with Guglielmo Trupia, was nominated for the best short film at the Raindance Film Festival 2013 and appears on http://vimeo.com/81617966.

What were you thinking?

JULIAN STANNARD

for Jack and William

ACKNOWLEDGEMENTS
Poems have appeared in the *TLS, Poetry Review, Manhattan Review, Ambit, Poetry, Salamander, Spectator, Poem, The Shop, The North, The Best British Poetry* (Salt, 2014), *A Mutual Friend: Poems for Charles Dickens* (Two Rivers Press, 2012) *The Twelve Poems of Christmas* (Candlestick Press, 2015). Twenty-one of these poems have appeared in a pamphlet called *The Street of Perfect Love* (Worple, 2014). A Hawthornden Fellowship in 2013 gave me the opportunity to write 'The Eau de Parfum of Mrs Radcliffe', and I am grateful for this.

First published in Great Britain in 2016
by CB editions
146 Percy Road London W12 9QL
www.cbeditions.com

All rights reserved

© Julian Stannard, 2016

The right of Julian Stannard to be identified
as author of this work has been asserted in accordance
with the Copyright, Designs and Patents Act, 1988

Printed in England by Blissetts, London W3 8DH

ISBN 978–1–909585–11–9

Contents

HAPPY

Dear All 3
Bus Replacement 4
Jerry Hall Meets Salvador Dalí 5
Alakefic 6
King's Cross 7
Émigrés 8
Retro-Catapult 9
Hermes 10
Karma 11
I'm Homesick for Being Homesick 12
Horizontal 13
Burlington Arcade 15
Cardiozal 16
Strokestown 17
Hampshire 18
Hell 19
Winston and Candy 22
Richard III, the Hindu King 23
The Water Stealer 25
Christ Stopped at Hollesley 27
September 1939 32
The Eau de Parfum of Mrs Radcliffe 34
Miss Pinkerton 42
Russell 43
Closed 46
La Douceur de la Nuit 47

THE STREET OF PERFECT LOVE

Chastity 51
Thigh-slapping on the Riviera 53

Dickens Discovers His Italian Babylon 55
Lorsica 58
Sleep in Lorsica 59
Stations of the Cross 60
Via Monte Bello 62
La Baia di Silenzio 63
Minestrone 64
Via Antonio Burlando 65
The Necropolis 67
Rimbaud in Milan 68
Napoli 70

DEAR NOSH

Breakfast with Tiffany 73
Lunch with Margot and Tinker 74
Lunch with Alex and Mildred 75
Lunch with Wendy and Lachlan 76
Lunch with Fleur 77
Eternal Lunch 78
Tea with Brenda and Charles 80
Buddhism 81
Supper in Lorsica 83
Happy Carp Christmas 84
Bohemian Horseradish 85
Beata and Stephen 88
The Gargantuan Muffin Beauty Contest 90
Donut 92
Dinner with Val 95
The Recipe 96

EAST FINCHLEY

East Finchley 99

HAPPY

Dear All

Just to let you know
the QMO document's been
converted to the intranet.

        Pam

(Phew!)

I could explode
with happiness.

Bus Replacement

What's the point of sitting on a bus
and fuming? For days I've been dragged

across the fringes of English cities
falling into melancholy and despair.

Sometimes we pass railway stations
and dream of journeys that are linear

and which are free from the humiliation
of chemical toilets and sick bags.

But what's the point of sitting on a bus
and fuming now that this one's

drifted into a crematorium?
We're getting out and stretching

legs, some of us are lying down
utterly defeated but almost happy.

Jerry Hall Meets Salvador Dalí

I flew to Paris at seventeen
and got talking to Jean-Paul
Sartre and Simone de Beauvoir
over coffee. I was happy
to meet them. The trouble is,
I just can't write poems
when I'm happy.

Mother said, The Riviera
is the place to go.
I bought a pink bikini,
some high-heeled shoes
and walked myself along the beach.

I love cooking, I love gardening.
I keep chickens. Mick's an alley cat.
Happy, happy, mostly happy.

Salvador Dalí said,
Why don't you run naked
through my sculpture garden?

Alakefic

I'm lying on a brown leather sofa
chatting to Mother on the phone.
Mother doesn't hear awfully well

but that doesn't stop her from talking.
Sometimes she says, What's that?
My mother likes the word 'ballistic'

as in I nearly went ballistic or Veronica
went ballistic or the Bude-Smiths went
ballistic. And she often says

'facetious': I hope you're not being . . .
And a lot of people have chips
on their shoulders which is bad

and woe betide mutton dressed as lamb.
And the word 'log' turns up quite a lot.
I'm down to my last log, she says,

do you think I should ring Neville?
I would, I say, lighting a cigarette.
You're not smoking!? she says.

Of course not! I've given smoking up!
I can hear my mother frowning.
And then she says, The trouble with

Neville is that he is so alakefic.
You're right about that, I say,
blowing smoke into the air.

King's Cross

When I lived in King's Cross
I used to lie on the bed and listen
to my bones melting. At first
I thought I was listening to Elgar
and then I thought I was listening
to the couple who'd moved
into the flat above and who were
getting to know each other better
and then I thought I was listening
to the music of the spheres.
I was listening to my bones melting.

Émigrés

Now that my neighbours
have returned to Poland

with their gaggle of children
and Mrs Grabowski making

one last indiscriminate visit
to the communal washing line

I think of sheets, my very own,
hanging somewhere in Gdansk.

Retro-Catapult

During medieval sieges
the assailants fired
plague-racked bodies
over ramparts.

Usually the person
had already expired
but if they hadn't
the long-range catapult
took care of that

especially if the calculations
went skew-whiff
and the body smashed
against a parapet.

Now they use
the long-range catapult
to catapult drugs
across the border.

Mexico City, Bogotá:
why not place an order?
Then walk across a lawn
cutting to the river
where the sun is always

shining, where fish
pop on the surface, where
the hummingbird hums
and hums and hums again.

Oh bird!

Hermes

Is this your first trip to the Cyclades?
Uncle Billy, he's my second cousin twice removed,
said now that I had some hair above my lip
it was time to visit the land of Petronius
and Aeschylus. Uncle Billy teaches Classics
so he's always coming up with shit like that.
He calls me Hermes, the path-finder, and says
he's going to buy me some golden sandals.

I like it here. Then I ate some toxic octopus:
I was feeling nauseous and slightly psychotic
but in a good kind of way, burning up inside.
Uncle Billy says if you're feeling horny
you need to act on it and the beaches are
driving me nuts. He doesn't mind I'm into girls
and there's this little group of senoritas
who take almost everything off.

Did I tell you uncle Billy's paying
for everything, a gift before I take up
post-grad work at UCL? Is UCL any good?
Thanks to the octopus and the Spanish
girls I just couldn't sleep so I asked Uncle Billy
for a Mogadon and he said, Hermes
prepare yourself for the dark side of the moon.
I'm feeling great now. Poetry? I'm mad for it.
Sometimes I lie down with uncle Billy
and we read poems to each other.
Do you like Rilke? Do you want me to stop?

Karma

Glenn Hoddle, perfect hair, astringent critic,
is saying, At the end of the day
the team which scores the most goals
wins. Put that way, I guess,
everything has a sudden clarity. Thank you!
And nice that Glenn is on Copacabana Beach:
hair moving in the breeze, blue shirt, tanned.
Half time: Germany nil, Algeria nil.
Any insightful thoughts? asks Gary Lineker.
Glenn clutches the microphone, The thing about
Aljazeera is that they've got nothing
to lose. Unless, says Lineker, their wing-backs
are languishing in some Egyptian jail.
Glenn looks bemused as if Lineker
has unearthed a metaphor that's too clever
for its own good. He pushes on: It's not just about
wing-backs, Gary, Aljazeera have got balls.

I'm Homesick for Being Homesick

It's time to dress up
in the clothes of the dead
is what Mother said
when she'd spent the afternoon
making chicken stock.

I wore my father's yellow socks
and my brother's moleskin trousers
and I lowered two feet into my
sister's husband's elongated
boots – the ones that marched back
from Moscow on their own.

I popped on a shirt worn by
an uncle who hanged himself
and I put into my pocket a couple of
linen handkerchiefs belonging
to the gamekeeper before he walked
over a cliff – and here's the hat which
sat so well on Jacob's head.

And a coat worn by Captain Catastrophe
before he keeled over with
an attack of charisma and don't forget
the scarf, my mother says, as she
drapes it around my neck.

It's chucking down.
Oh good! I gather the lurchers
the smooth-haired lurchers
and stride across the heath.

Horizontal

I'm sick of being an upright green bin
full of the crap you chuck in my mouth.
In any case I'm an adolescent green bin
and I write poetry so I want to spend
a great deal of my time in the horizontal
position. When the wind blows I let
myself get thrown around the provinces
emptying gunk on the sodden streets.
If I end up in some cul-de-sac I'm happy!
Il faut être absolument horizontal.

I blow around Southampton
which I pronounce in a French accent
to buzz things up. Sometimes I bump
into bins of a similar disposition schooled
in the Parnassian tradition but eager
to transgress. Sometimes I'm as terrified
as 76,000 new-born pups,
other times my tongue un-cleaves itself
and I'm uncontrollably scatological. Mother's
going mad calling in social workers
and ringing the police. I can't say enough

about this new-style horizontal vagabondaggio.
I will not be God's little donkey!
Once I blew as far as Paris and fell in with
a bunch of soldiers. Something happened.
Sometimes I fetch up in London – that gorgeous
godless city. For a while I lived in Camden
in a somewhat chaotic same-bin relationship.

When I got back to Southampton,
or rather *Southâmptòn*, Mother went crazy.
She needs to modernise, she doesn't like it one bit
when I say, God is one mighty shit.

Never mind. Look at me now, the horizontal green bin
blowing off to Addis Ababa, *voilà, voilà*.

Burlington Arcade

I'm being carried down
the Burlington Arcade
by Beadles in top hats,
jewellers on both sides
holding out their hands
and wrapped in cashmere.
When people speak of
near-death experiences
they're always going through
tunnels, they're happy,
they're never going through
the Burlington Arcade.

Eric says, It's good
to see you wearing clothes
and I have to admit he's
wearing the most beautiful
trousers and I say, Eric
you're not supposed to be
in this poem. Get back
into your shop! I can see
a light at the end of the tunnel.
The Head Beadle's saying
'Burlington Gardens!'

Should I tip him?
Am I dead?
What happens next?

Cardiozal

Leonora Carrington

I didn't want to end up
in a Spanish lunatic asylum
on Cardiozal and in such filth,
Max already in America
and me floating around
with several holes in my head.
Wrote to Peggy Guggenheim,
but not a stamp in sight.

Nanny turned up
in a submarine
which I painted red
and off we went:

playing cribbage
deliriously happy
or at least not unhappy.

Strokestown

Co. Roscommon

Sunlight breaks the clouds
and the sheep are singing
Here Comes the Sun
and when I say singing I mean
bleating but one of the sheep
looks like George Harrison
and the difference between
a bleat and a song and
the difference between
a legend and a sheep
I'm not going to ruin the day
by splitting hairs.

I walk out of the Big House
with a tartan rug
and lay it down among
the choir of sheep and I lie
on the rug to gape at the sky.
The sheep are looking at me
in a most encouraging way.
The sheep are hoping for
a revelation, something
they can pass around themselves
so I turn to them and say
This is the nearest I've been
             to America.

Hampshire

When you drive me
into Hampshire
it always seems
you're taking me to bed:

a king-sized bed
involving vast amounts
of goose feather!

When you drive me
into Hampshire
cows stand in the mist

and swans loop on the river.
Let's stop the car!
Let's find a glade,

a cavalry of bluebells.
I'll make the crook
of my arm into a pillow.

Hell

I've been in hell a while now and it's not too bad.
Sure, I was nervous enough the first day:
you can just imagine, all those people milling around.
It reminded me of public school somehow:
not knowing who was going to burst through the bog door.
We had to strip but they gave us clean towels
which was rather more civilised than I'd imagined.

And that was that, you just had to keep walking
down labyrinthine corridors listening to snatches of
what seemed to be a re-worked version of the Pet Shop Boys.
It was so dark but I suppose that's the whole point
and sometimes you end up in what I can only describe
as a steam room, smelling vaguely of eucalyptus oil.
I thought only asphodels would grow down here.

When the Prince of Darkness and his equipage walk through
it's backs to the wall, only here the walls seem
to be made from flesh, it's difficult to explain really;
you're left dangling in that superannuated air.
Sometimes you're allowed a little amyl nitrate
which incinerates your nostrils and gives you quite a charge.
It's like holding onto a doodlebug.

Are only men sent to hell? I haven't seen any women yet.
It never crossed my mind that hell was just for blokes.
Maybe the girls have got their own place:
cleaner toilets, potpourris and the cushions all pumped up.
Perhaps Beelzebub will organise the occasional soirée
with bottles of *Lachryma Christi* and a real knees-up.
Right now women seem like a Hollywood script.

But even in hell there are moments of respite:
you spend hours pushing through the corridors of darkness
and break into a pool of muscular youths.
It looks as if they been chiselled out of alabaster
and they're so well hung! As a rule I find
damnation's good for the figure. I'm pleased with the result.
Everyone's fascinated by reflections.

You never know who you're going to meet down here.
I've seen a lot of Rimbaud and Verlaine.
They call them Arthur and Martha and they're always at it
but they carry it off with a certain panache
and if they like you they're generous with the absinthe:
everything gets quite jolly, reciting poems and stuff
in a weird French. Auden's another matter.

You should see his face! A wedding cake left out in the rain.
That was a good day! Here it's a cake on a Bunsen burner.
He spends most of the time saying bugger off
not that people need much encouragement.
I think he's lost his marbles or had them yanked
which seems unfair given his age and general demeanour.
He has some great stories about Berlin.

After a while you start getting institutionalised.
There's a certain amount of tetchiness and towel thieving.
Actually it's about time they handed out some new ones.
Not sure who you suck up to, or suck off, to get another.
You can probably get one on the black market.
It seems to me a lot of the damned prefer to go naked
which is why the devils are fond of pitchforks.

There's a lot of irritating bureaucracy too
which is designed to give people something to think about
otherwise they'd really go out of their minds
but there's a general consensus that

the Inferno is becoming increasingly Italianised.
If you know the guy in charge of the sauna it's hey presto
and you go straight to the front of the queue.

We thought it was going to be an adventure
but it turns out that hell's becoming a bit of a bore.
It's true Foucault's doing a little French conversation
and they're talking about alternative Bible classes.
And there was quite a stir when a peculiar aristocrat
set up a rock group and called it Citizen Sade.
Great for a while but we found it irksome

trying to dance with our ankles tethered to a goat.
And the food *so* drab. All we get is oxtail soup.
We tried sending round a petition but nothing came of it.
What I'd give for an apple and a piece of cheese!
The story around here is that the old gentleman's
sloped off. He was having quite a problem with his nerves
and was somewhat depressed and, well, knackered.

These days Nick sends over weekly instructions.
I'd say hell's suffering from a lack of leadership
and the devilry has definitely lost its chutzpah.
They're not really putting their backs into it:
the fires are burning low and sometimes it's not even hot.
Our season in hell is turning mild.
Of an evening we get together and listen to a nightingale.

All in all a disappointment.
We thought we were at one of the hottest shows in town
and it's turning out to be all smoke and mirrors.
Nox Perpetuum has become *Nox Tedium*.
Rimbaud and Verlaine are asleep most of the time,
the Pet Shop Boys have lost their groove.
Please, someone give us a break, turn on the light.

Winston and Candy

I was walking along the banks of the River Yangtze
suffused with delicious feelings of cherry blossom.
Winston gripped my elbow and whispered,
Candy, one day we could put down a deposit on a horse.
My heart skipped and I was giddy enough to kiss him!

I am Candy and Winston has dreams of being my lover.
He is as loyal as a dog and I can't tell you how ugly he is.
I'm going to talk about China's over-heated horse market.
Foreigners scatter their money. Macroeconomics!
Chairman Deng said getting rich was glorious.

Big horse, little horse, who gives a fuck about mice.
Kung says, I love my wife, I love my horse, my horse is quiet.
I told Winston, Change your reading habits, *exercise!*
Affordable horses are on the decline! People are marching.
We are millions! I hear horses cantering over the plains.

What is that sound high in the air? Genghis? Buddha?
Now the government is restricting horse credit.
You keep a horse five years, you pay less tax.
You buy two horses, they throw your baby in the lake.
The unflinching discipline of our revolving emperors!

Richard III, the Hindu King

The Hindu from Leicester is smiling:
This is a good day for the city, it will put
Leicester on the map for ever, the entire world
is looking at Leicester.
I'm already feeling slightly bored.
A business opportunity, he says.
A Hindu entrepreneur with an interest
in the Plantagenets. The woman in the wheelchair
is saying Richard was given a bad press
because he was a hunchback but he wasn't –
just a bit crooked, but then who isn't?
King Richard III, the Patron Saint of Hunchbacks.
A good day for disability rights, the woman says.
And a good day for Hindus, says the Hindu.
And a good day for car parks, says the car park.

Richard Coles is singing

           Don't Leave Me This Way

which is what Richard III has been singing too.
You could hear him during the night –
the last great medieval lamentation.
Richard Coles feels close to Richard
because he's called Richard and Richard Coles,
the ex-Communard in a dog collar,
is making a large pot of soup
which everyone can share:
several cardamom pods, a pinch of garam masala.
The cortège is now passing Ladbrokes –
a horse shits on the road.

Academics from Liverpool are saying
Richard III was blond and blue-eyed,
a poster boy for the Plantagenets.
Richard Coles is stirring his aromatic soup.
The expert on Richard III has grown wings.
Richard was a pious man, she says,
who has suffered five hundred years of abuse –
his nephews were actually miniature troubadours
who sailed with Columbus
and once they got to the New World
they wrote a book. She's holding the book.
To be a medieval historian is bliss.
And they went to India too, says the Hindu.

The Water Stealer

The poet says
I'm going to read
a poem called
'The Water Stealer'
and then he shuffles
his papers; he
can't find the poem
so he shuffles
his papers a little more.
An ancient Greek
tale, he says
una filostrocca –
flick–flack–flick:
all we can hear
is the sound of paper:
almost, in a way,
a tango, which is not
a tango (how could it,
in all honesty,
be a tango?), we are
miles from Buenos Aires
and not a violin
nor a double bass
in sight, only
a white-haired poet
looking for a poem
which is buried
among the poems
he doesn't want
to read: flick–flack–flick.
He wants to read

'The Water-Stealer'.
Maybe, he says.
someone's stolen
the poem and we laugh
because he wants us
to laugh and we feel bad
that he can't find
his poem. Or maybe,
and now his throat
makes a noise
which sounds like
a wind – a
wind climbing up
a trouser leg
on the west coast of
Ireland – I haven't
written the poem yet

Christ Stopped at Hollesley

My mother asked me
to take a turkey
to my sister who lives
on the other side
of the heath.

Mother said,
Your sister lives
on the other side
of the heath.

Thank you Mother
I have known that
for the entirety of my life.

Good, she said.

I am the Alpha
and I am the Omega
I am the turkey bearer.

Give me a truly
enormous turkey
and I will take it across the heath.

Here it is, my mother said,
and then, uncharacteristically,
she broke into French, *Voilà* –
a truly enormous turkey
to carry across the heath.

Oh thank you, I said
thank you, thank you, thank you!

Everybody's gone into the light
other than my sister, who lives
on the heath, my mother with her
unassailable position vis-à-vis
the management of logs and me –
the Alpha, the Omega, the bearer
of turkeys, etcetera, etcetera.

So I carry the turkey across
the heath because tomorrow
is Christmas and everybody's going
into the light, apart from
the Three Musketeers
of which I am one, the other two
being my unconquerable mother
who watched the Battle of Britain
and thrust a pitchfork or two
into parachuting Germans,
and sister mine who liveth on the heath.

Good luck my child,
who carries a turkey
in the dead of night
on the eve of Christmas
stars in the sky, the wise
men mixing up a little
camel food just in case
they are called upon
to cross a desert or even,
God forbid, a heath
and baby Jesus, let's not
forget about him, the size
and weight of a tiny turkey.

Good luck my child,
good luck. Take some
glühwein for a little luck.

My mother, who has an
eye for detail, put the turkey
on a tray and oiled up
the rifle in the shed.

The stars are out
the owls are hooting
a sharp wind off the sea.
All I have to do – now
that I'm carrying a
turkey on a tray across
a heath – is not fall
over and not be attacked
by an axe man with a
golden axe. All I have
to do is take the turkey
the size of Jesus junior
to my sister's house
on the other side of
the oyster-catching heath
where the moon is breaking
free of the clouds
and the heath has an orange
glow: I can see rabbits
at an end-of-season champagne
dinner dance: I can see
waves cascading off
the turkey – *whoosh!*
I can see Jesus standing
in a glade surrounded

by deer. He is a man
aged 33, a man with
bodily parts. He appears
to be holding
a beard trimmer.

You who are carrying
an enormous turkey
the size of holy Jesus,
account for yourself.

And I have a terrible
recollection of being
a schoolboy tiptoeing
into the school kitchens
where all the turkeys
were laid out like hopeful
virgins (bless the Lord!).
They gave us bromide
but sometimes the bromide
didn't work. We carried
the turkeys down
infinite corridors –
we were awfully hungry.

O sister, here is the turkey
our *felix culpa*. I have had
a fright – I saw Jesus on
the heath with a beard trimmer.
Ah, a beard trimmer, says
my sister. Yes. Here it is,
the turkey that is,
that we will eat tomorrow.
Can you cook it? Yes,
she says, and then:

Oh brother, welcome
to the house of the dead
the Alpha, the Omega,
the beginning and the end,
a turkey the size of Jesus
who takes away the sins
of the world, the resurrection
and the eternal life to come.

Oh sister, I said.

September 1939

London seems peaceful
and rather empty.
I think we're going to be okay.
I'm feeling almost happy.
I think we should get married
or have some kind of affair.
I think we should have a holiday:
Devon maybe, can't go to Berlin!
I wonder what they're saying
on the Kurfürstendamm? I'm going
to write to Heinrich and say
This war shouldn't make
the blindest bit of difference.
Oh, what do you think?
I think we should dress down
and make a habit of undressing
a little more often than we do.
Come, let me help you.
I think we should go to the Ritz
and really splash out.
I think we should pretend
we can't sleep because
of the nightingales.
I think we should sing
There'll Always Be an England
and just when we've got the hang
of it we should suddenly stop
and look away.

I think we should bruise our
mouths with damsons.
I think we should listen to jazz
and move our bodies like this.
I think I'll wear that cardigan
which makes me feel slightly odd.
I think we should go to that restaurant
in Dean Street. I think I'm going
to throw my arms around you
and hold you a little more tightly
than I normally hold you
and you're going to say:
Please stop, you're hurting me!
I think we should listen to the wireless.
I think we should lie for hours
in a field and look at the sky.

The Eau de Parfum of Mrs Radcliffe

Imagine a castle defended by poets.
How easily we capitulated!
The first cannon ball was enough
to send us into a collective funk
though the American lesbian managed
to stand on the parapet and yell
in a blood-curdling way for a while.

Our enemies – who exactly were they? –
were unimpressed by their victory.
They made us stay at the castle
and write poems in praise of defeat.

Boxes of food are left outside
the kitchen door and more or less
we fend for ourselves, though
we have the use of a cook called Hemingway
and Mary the housekeeper whose
Midlothian vowels make the animals
                              twitch.

Sometimes some middle-ranking officer
dines with us, bringing some decent wine
and the cook conjures up
something reasonable and we have
to read our poems of subjugation.
The man with the stripe down his leg
leans back in the baronial chair with
a quixotic look, smoking an acrid cigar.

When they lock the narrow door
and all attempts to make thistle wine
dwindle into catatonic listlessness
we retire to our rooms to compose.

I had not realised how much
one could look at a tree and hate it.

The lesbian poet sobs continuously.
Apart from the housekeeper
there are only men here:

she must be lonely –

Week after week:
a castle of poets crushed,
occupied, abandoned,
humiliated. Does humiliation
breed a special kind of love?

Poets disappear –
dragged off to a freak show
or lined up against the courtyard wall
and shot, their poems,
according to the commissar,
guilty of a *jouissance*
that creeps into the writing
notwithstanding everything.

We pass round
the lugubrious cordial
willing our poems
to sink deeper

and deeper

and

For a while
there were six of us
but the middle-aged Italian
died of a broken heart
and the young poet
from Basingstoke threw
himself down a ravine.

A little more food
to go round and two
empty chairs –
could we use them for firewood?

Ah, the hour of tea.
Try some Verlaine!

My earnest neighbour
many a night
lets out a loud, troubling wail
his sleeplessness
is a kind of drug.
These sufferings
from other rooms
are what dreams are
made of.
He takes his solace
from the wildlife.

I have seen him
in the study
gazing rhapsodically
across the valley.
His book full of beautifully
written stanzas
in praise of the falcon,
his cheeks wet.

Oh danger, danger.

The castle creaks and groans
footsteps in the corridors,
a lavatory half-flushed,
a rattling key

and Mrs Radcliffe's
shockingly beautiful
       Eau de Parfum.

One night I met the American poet
on the stairs by candlelight.
How much self-hate can there be? she asked.
I said, There can always be a little more.

And there's a poet called Jacob
who likes to wear a suit.
He's short and neat and taciturn
and is becoming balder by the day,
we never enter a poet's room
because that would be as if one were
putting a hand into the flame without

ever getting the chance to take it out.
Last night Jacob knocked on my door
(he looked so small!) and thrust a poem
at me. Oh, my heart was beating!
It was magnificent, and it was horrible
such sensuous tropes: such ardour,
such languor, such candour, such . . .

I was envious that the muscles
of his heart were in perfect order.

He asked me to destroy it
and I put the poem in the sink
(oh look away!) and lit it
     with a match.

When the rain went
and the sky cleared
and the sun shone
they sent a boy
to cut the grass –
a lovely boy!

He had a machine
which he rode across the fields
followed by a dog.

For a day, the castle smelt
of cut grass, our hearts were giddy.

Such fragrance, such hope.
Let's put a stop to that!

Hemingway
took a pistol to his head

and shot himself
but the pistol was empty
thank goodness for that:
more soup, more boiled ham.
One day he pulled a trout
out of the river.

The only time
he smiled
was when he proposed
a round of Scottish roulette
a game which involves
a vast amount of porridge.
I really can't say any more.

The days are getting longer.
Light through the valley.
Badgers bumping into badgers.

Jacob's dark suit
has become a raven
he flies to the wood,

a gift!

A bagpipe in the turret.
Did you hear it? A wound?
A warning? Nothing.

The man with the stripe
down his leg
doesn't come any more.
Our poems bored him.
Our poems bore us.

Shall we write a poem
to the longest day?

Oh let's not!

There's drumbeat
in the hills, and gunfire.

Are they planning
to lay siege to the castle again?
A castle defended
by three poets
a housekeeper
and a neurasthenic cook.

Who will stand
in front of the cannon ball?

Who will win the poetry prize?

I think the housekeeper
has turned into a sparrow.
Look, there she goes!

I think Hemingway
has turned into a fish.
Let's put him in the river.

Have you not thought
how quiet the castle is?
Birdsong, stag leap, wild flowers.

I think the soldiers have gone.
I think the soldiers were never here.

Gracious lesbian, honest rhapsodist,
stop writing and be of good cheer.

The narrow door is open
and there's a long drive
in which anything could happen
and at the end of the drive
there are gates, which
even as we speak, are opening.

Shall we walk along it?

Miss Pinkerton

Sometimes I wake in the early hours
and worry about Miss Pinkerton.
Letters for her are piling up in the hallway,
I think of her making an Irish stew
and forking an excellent dumpling.
I see her opening the wardrobe and saying no to a dress,
sex is not without a dose of stress.
What can a girl do with skin so pale?
Sometimes Miss Pinkerton runs naked from the bathroom
and cartwheels above my ceiling.

Sometimes I wake in the early hours
and ponder upon Miss Pinkerton.
Letters for her are piling up in the hallway,
I think of her eating a sticky pudding
and dabbing her eyes with a cucumber.
I see her opening her wardrobe and looking for leather,
I think Miss Pinkerton awfully clever.
What can a girl do with such Pre-Raphaelite hair?
Sometimes Miss Pinkerton runs naked from the bathroom
and sings Could You, Could You be Loved.

Sometimes I wake in the early hours
and contemplate Miss Pinkerton.
Letters for her are piling up in the hallway,
I think of her boiling a gorgeous ham
and throwing salt over her shoulder.
I see her opening the wardrobe and choosing a whip,
I think Miss Pinkerton a little hip.
What can a girl do with such libido?
Sometimes Miss Pinkerton runs naked from the bathroom
and taps upon my door like this

Russell

Southampton General Hospital

And when we came back from
the Caribbean after a five week
cruise neither of our cars worked.
They said it was the battery and
I thought it can't be the battery
but they continued to say that it was.
Anyway, listen to this, a couple
of days later I got the Mercedes
to work – it was probably
because we'd been away so long.
We're often doing that, going off
somewhere, and then coming back.
– Get away much?

No, I wanted to say but I wasn't
quick enough: Russell continued:
Cars don't like not being driven
that's my opinion, not that I'm
a mechanic or anything but I do
appreciate cars, they're not dissimilar
to women: you've got to know
how to handle them, when to put your
foot down, no dilly-dallying
with the clutch – What do you drive?

Actually . . .
So I took it back for an MOT
and the man said ninety-five
and I said I never pay more than
fifty – Russell winked –

and just like that the man said
Okay, fifty, and he drove it
back to the house when it was done.
What car did you say you had?
I don't. What? I don't have a car.

Wow! said Russell.
And I wanted to reach over
covered as he was in plaster casts
and a gash across his face
and his eyes bloodshot and
hug him gently.
I wanted to say I have listened
to you for days:
you are an unforgettable part
of my hospital experience:

you have not hesitated
in sending words along the one-way
motorway which connects our beds.
When I leave the hospital,
I will find a moment to say very quietly
Oh Russell – notwithstanding
everything – never will you be
a bolt of silk in a starburst of light.

I wanted to say, Thank you:
I now know everything
you can possibly know about
the Portakabin business.
It was ridiculous of me to spend
so long in a Portakabin void.

Russell, I said, it's a miracle
you're alive! Knocked off

your bicycle by a car in the
New Forest and the car (no,
don't ask) fast and overtaking
and head on – slam. Yes, said Russell
I suppose I should be happy
I'm not dead. We're all happy
I said. Russell looked a little sad
but then he smiled – the John Coltrane
of Portakabins smiled.

Why did I say John Coltrane?
He doesn't even like John Coltrane.
Are you in any pain? I asked.
No, said Russell, not in any pain
whatsoever, not even a twinge.

Because, I said, you have handed
all your pain to me,
and I can feel every damn bit of it
and oddly enough I'm happy
as if Jesus had hopped from your shoulder
onto mine, the Jesus who walked
in the Garden of Gethsemane,
the Jesus who took out a little time
to harrow hell, the Jesus who said
Why have you forsaken me?

Oh goodness, said Russell, I'm sorry.
Don't be – I want you to be mended.
That's why we're here, he said
to be mended, and he was laughing.
That's why we're here, I said.

Mend us!

Closed

The next station is Closed
which is exactly where I want to be:
it takes a while to get out
but eventually I find a bus
called Not In Service:
it's on the other side of the river
property is cheap
and there are Pleasure Gardens
which nobody visits
and a Bed and Breakfast called
No Vacancies (perfect!).
There's an ATM which never works
and a kebab shop.
A lot of people are cross-eyed
and the Protestant Work Ethic
is a weird sex club
which I'd recommend, mostly.

La Douceur de la Nuit

The refuse collectors
have been on strike for weeks.
I have never been so happy.

Bins have learnt to move
their hips. I've seen them
throbbing in the moonlight.

Have you heard
Cesária Évora's mournful song
to uncollected bins?

The rats link arms and
dance with melancholy
and the cats have

turned themselves
into aromatic troubadours.
When I open the window

pungent fruit leaps
onto my bed and the black sacks
sway like belly palms.

THE STREET OF PERFECT LOVE

Chastity

Although I'd long sunk
into Jim's unwashed sheets
finding myself in a state of
existence known as sleeping
I was conscious of a dark shape
clanking glasses which
turned out to be none other
than Jim himself who didn't
like to drink alone but who
would if there was no one
around to oblige him.
How can you sleep like that,
he said, after writing
a poem of that strange ilk?
And he recited the poem to me
which contained the words:
slipping off into the far corners
of the metropolitana.

Jim, I said, it's the middle of
the night and tomorrow
I must go to the Palace of Justice.
It's because you must go to the Palace of Justice
I'm clanking these glasses, he said.
And he turned on the one functioning
bulb in that unimaginable Profundis.
And we need to talk about that
box of After Eights you gave to Phyllis.
Jim, I said, it was only a box of chocolates.

Well, I've never seen such a phallic box
of chocolates, Jim said, and I said

I've never considered
that After Eights could be anything other
than a spur to chastity.
Well, said Jim, if you weren't a literary man
I'd beat the shit out of you.

We drank under that naked bulb
till the dawn broke
and Genoese sparrows threw themselves
against the windows, only the windows
were broken so the sparrows
flew in and crapped in the corners.
Jim's head had fallen onto his chest
and I threw a jacket around my shoulders
and ran to the Palace of Justice.

When I got there
I saw that my estranged wife
had attached herself to a megaphone,
not that she needed one (at least
that was my view).

Thigh-slapping on the Riviera

I was at the Town Hall
in Rapallo, trying
to find something out.
The concierge
a man with a moustache
said, *Sono ignorante
non so niente*,
I call the Dottoressa.
When the Dottoressa came
she said You must be
our German scholar.
The Dottoressa
linked arms and took me
this way and that way
– her German scholar –
down marble corridors
into painted rooms.

When we met
her colleagues
she said, Here is
the German scholar
and as the sun soared
I practised clicking
my heels and found
that it came quite easily:
so I clicked this way
and clicked that way
and clicked across
the courtyard
in front of the mayor

and sometimes I stooped
to kiss a hand,
a lady's hand I ought to add.
We German scholars
like a little hand.

Oh look at the German scholar
(how could I say I was English!).
They wanted a bit of clicking
and my God I was giving it to them.
A click here, a click there
a sudden stoop,
I was reviving the old clicking alliance.
They had their Mare Nostrum,
I had a pair of heels.

Dickens Discovers His Italian Babylon

In the course of two months
the flitting shapes and shadows
of my dismal entering reverie
gradually resolved themselves
into familiar forms and substances

and I already began to think
that when the time should come
for closing the long holiday
and turning back to England
I might part from Genoa with

anything but a glad heart.
It is a place that *grows upon you*
every day. There seems to be
always something to find out.
There are the most extraordinary

alleys and by-ways to walk about in.
You can lose your way (what a comfort
that is, when you are idle!) twenty
times a day. It abounds in
the strangest contrasts: things that

are picturesque, ugly, mean,
magnificent, delightful and offensive
break upon the view at every turn.
The houses are immensely high
painted in all sorts of colours

and are in every stage of damage,
dirt and lack of repair.
As it is impossible for coaches

to penetrate into these streets
there are sedan chairs, gilded

and otherwise, for hire in divers
places. I had earlier made
the mistake of asking the whip
to take me to Piazza San Bernardo.
The young women are not generally

pretty but they walk remarkably well.
I had earlier made the mistake
of asking the whip to take me
to an apothecary. The women are not
generally pretty but oh they walk

remarkably well. How shall I forget
the Streets of Palaces: Strada Nuova
and Via Balbi!: the great, heavy, stone
balconies, one above another, and
tier over tier: with here and there,
one larger than the rest, towering
high up – a huge marble platform;
the doorless vestibules, massively
barred lower windows, immense
public staircases, thick marble pillars,
strong dungeon-like arches, and
dreary, dreaming, echoing vaulted
chambers: among which the eye
wanders again, and again, and again
as every palace is succeeded by another
– the terrace gardens between house
and house, with green arches of
the vine, and groves of orange trees
and blushing oleander in full bloom

twenty, thirty, forty feet above
the street. The steep up-hill streets
of small palaces with marble terraces
looking down into close by-ways –
the magnificent and innumerable
churches; and the rapid passage
from a street of stately edifices
into a maze of the vilest squalor,
steaming with unwholesome stenches
and swarming with half-naked
children and whole worlds of
dirty people – make up, altogether,
such a scene of wonder: so lively
and yet so dead: so noisy and yet
so quiet: so obtrusive, and yet
so shy and lowering: so wide awake
and yet so fast asleep: that is
a sort of intoxication to a stranger
to walk on, and on, and on, and
look about him. A bewildering
phantasmagoria, with all the
inconsistency of a dream and all
the pain and all the pleasure
of an extravagant reality!

I made the mistake of asking
the whip to take me
to Vico dell' Amor Perfetto.
The women are not generally
pretty but oh but oh but oh
they do walk remarkably well.

Lorsica

When the storm came
they were taken out of themselves
and no one saw that the boys
had gone up with the cows
and when night fell you could see
torchlight on the slopes of Ramaceto

and they were saying they would
find them cowering and safe
and when they got to the stone house
they found that the boys had been struck
by lightning and the cows were dead too
and Enzo shouted across the valley
Morti, i ragazzi sono morti!

and Gabriella who had waited
for her sons to return from the war
only to have them killed
on the slopes of Ramaceto
started to scream and the valley
explored every angle of her grief

and when the sun rose there were olives
and grapes and there were drooling dogs
and Angelo and Fillipo were yellow birds
gripping the tiles of their mother's roof

Sleep in Lorsica

What are we going to do
when we are old
living in Lorsica
plucking a peach from
Signora Volpone's
peach tree
listening to the cicada
and making the annual
coach trip to Mussolini's grave
even if our fathers fought
in the resistance, even if
we are card-carrying members
of the Communist Party?

To live apart from the world
is to suffer a peculiar ecstasy.
The chestnut tree is the tree
        of life
and blue toad sings reptilian Fado
which makes the cats
dance an exquisitely melancholic
        dance.

Let us look at the mountains
and then let us close the shutters,
let us lie on the slate floor
and have Sebastian the dog
lick us into everlasting sleep.

Stations of the Cross

Someone had taken an axe
to my life which meant
that although everything
was in pieces we needed
a Christmas tree
if only for the children
to gather round as they listened
to a wound-up version of
Stille Nacht, Heilige Nacht.

Someone had taken an axe
to the forest – now there were
Christmas trees throughout the city.
Lucky me! I took myself
to the Mercato Orientale
to pick up my tree
and screw down the thorns
because someone had
taken an axe to my life.

I picked up my Christmas tree
and carried it all the way
to our house on the hill
which had turned into
an outpost of hell but
even hell wants a Christmas tree
UN ALBERO DI NATALE.

I carried my tree
past the Hotel Metropoli
I carried my tree
to Saint Anna's Funicular.
Oh, they said,

it's St Julian the leper
Julian of the *mot juste*
Julian with an axe in his head
carrying a Christmas tree
to an outpost of hell.

Sometimes people swung
a punch
just for the hell of it.
Someone started hammering
a nail into my head
just for the hell of it.
Evidently
I had done something wrong!
Then I carried my tree along
Corso Magenta where the blind man
turned a blind eye.

And I carried my tree
up Salita Santa Maria della Sanità
and I carried my tree to the eighth floor
because the lift was broken
and the woman who'd taken an axe
to my life said, Ah, un albero di natale,
we've been waiting so fucking long
for un albero di natale.

Put it there in the corner.
Careful, careful.
Oh look it's beautiful,
a little red perhaps
but beautiful. Here's a cloth
to wipe your face.
You'll frighten the children.
They'll think you've gone mad.

Via Monte Bello

The lampshade
hanging from

the ceiling
is Eleanor

of Aquitaine
kneeling

La Baia di Silenzio

I lay myself down
in the Bay of Silence.
The wind kicked up
and scudded across
the sea. The wind
got into the rigging
and the Bay of Silence
wasn't silent at all
with sails flapping
like scarecrows
on the threshold of
delirium. A girl
shrieked. Something
was coming off
the sea which
could only be death
or the sister of death
or the cocktail of
death or the methadone
of death or the
ecstasy of death
or the aftershave
of death or the sweet
morning feeling
of death, or the hit me,
hit me, hit me
of death, or the *la la la*
of death. Goodbye.

Minestrone

When I telephone
my erstwhile inamorata
she speaks in the voice
of minestrone. Not the minestrone
her mother would make
having stood the entire morning
in a small windowless kitchen
throwing diced vegetables
into a pot whilst intoning
Giacomo Leopardi's
The Approach of Death.

No, it is not that voice.
Nor does the voice say:
I could rustle up a scallopina,
some grilled aubergines
and a salad so fresh and delectable
you would glow, *mio caro*, you would glow!

No, the voice is the voice
of a minestrone hunkering down
at the bottom of the pot:
it's thick and beginning to congeal,
it will probably do for another day.

I could warm it up, *mio caro bello*,
and scrape it out with a spoon
and serve it to you in a bowl
whose hair-line crack has formed
two distinct geographical kingdoms.
I could do all of this for you
because once upon a time
do you remember? – you were my husband.

Via Antonio Burlando

Don't go there. Not today:
October 11th, when the sky
is as thick as a minestrone
you would never want to eat
even if you were feeling peckish.

Tell me why I'm in this flat
in Via Antonio Burlando
where every chandelier
        has a single bulb.

I'm standing on the poggiolo
letting the rain drench me.
Rain – that schoolboy ballad
which Edward Thomas sang.
He heard the Angel of Death
in that frozen barracks. Mud on
his boots, Ovaltine comforter.

I'm eight floors up. I could die
in a moment. I could throw
myself into the River Bisagno
which is a river without water
whose occupants are rats
        the size of horses.

I can see the stadium
        the prison
              the necropolis.

And they smoke when they deal the cards
in the bars of Via Antonio Burlando
ignoring the VIETATO FUMARE

the butcher serving nerve ends
Colonel Burlando bright-eyed on the night bus.
The Farmacia sells only suppositories.
The fishmonger can get hold of a fish
which will send us into ecstasies.

October 12th, the colour of the city has changed.
With a little eye-stretching you can
see the sea hovering below the sky:
Via Antonio Burlando, we're on the
offal side of the city, valleys break
into the hinterland, a police siren has
replaced the sound of rain. I'm eight floors
up smoking a cigarette on a poggiolo
        which shakes in the wind.

The Necropolis

When I walked into the necropolis
at Genoa I saw that every grave

had been allocated a panettone
and because the Council was in

broad terms a coalition of the left
every panettone was in a red box

and because every panettone
was in a red box I had a hunch

the old Maoist-Leninist-Stalinist
front were calling a meeting

with the dead and because the
dead were bored of being dead

they clapped and shouted
like nuns who have discovered

the libido and because nuns
have discovered the libido

I am going to bring the poem
to a sudden end. Sleep well!

Rimbaud in Milan

I look like a kid
but I'm a hundred and fifty-nine
and one of my legs has gone missing.
I don't have a pension plan
and all the money I ever made
went somewhere else. I is someone else.
J'ai faim, HO FAME. I'm famous.
See this mongrel, it's Verlaine.
Sometimes we read poems
to each other but they sound
strange and I don't even like them.
I'm down on my luck in Milan
Maman's looking for me
and yes I've got lice in my hair,
I'm rather fond of them.

Can you help me? JE EST UN AUTRE.
I'm awfully hungry, I'm pretty sure
life isn't here, it's somewhere else.
Sometimes they use me as a mannequin –
this is, after all, the city of mannequins –
dragging me across the floor of
DOLCE & GABBANA. *C'est drôle*:
the one-legged poet mannequin
who doesn't know how to die
who knows how to hop beautifully.
Oh hop with me to the barricades!
I is Rimbaud, HO FAME.
I have the mendicant's obligatory

hound, I have already explained.
Mon cher Verlaine, mon frère,
I haven't written a poem for years.
In fact, I don't really like poems.

Napoli

The boat was beating across the bay,
we had our backs to Vesuvius,
the wind smacked our faces.
Naples was an enormous packet of cigarettes
you could smoke until you conked out:
the cigarettes were never going to run out
and nor was the coffee, the drugs,
the prostitutes, the locked churches,
the scooters, the rice cakes, the evil eye,
the boys called Gennaro, the funiculars,
the shrines to Madonna, the shrines
to Maradona, the bullet holes, the heat,
the permanent state of crucifixion.
Anyone could be crucified two thousand
years ago but to be crucified now,
to be crucified in Napoli – lift me up!

DEAR NOSH

Breakfast with Tiffany

How are you feeling, Tiff?
Actually, I'm feeling a little sore.
Oh, I'm feeling a little stiff.

Lunch with Margot and Tinker

My stepfather the Duke of Bonheur
was twenty-nine
steps removed from
the Marquis de Sade
so I was beaten an awful lot
 said Tinker.

Anyway, said Margot
in that impeccable English,
my father flew Junkers in the war
and he always had a plane
with enough fuel
to fly Hitler to Brazil.

 Tinker said:
Are you old enough
to remember
Sputniks over London?

Oh what a pity,
it was marvellous and
at the end of the street
there was a bunker.

 Margot said:
Can you imagine climbing
out of the bunker and looking
left and then looking right
and seeing nothing?

Lunch with Alex and Mildred

It's my birthday, Alex said
let's have lunch at the Hôtel de Paris.

The Bentley came round
to the flat in Cannes
and we motored off to Monte Carlo.

I could hear my flip-flops
as I flip-flopped across the marble floor.

Oh, Mildred said, sucking on
a langoustine, it's Roger Moore.

Who darling? *Roger Moore!*
What's that darling?

ROGER ROGER FUCKING MOORE!
Alex said, Would you like a little more?

Lunch with Wendy and Lachlan

He told me that half
the Mackinnons were killed
at Culloden.

Then, continued Wendy,
(we were eating lamb!)
he said he was related
to Bonnie Prince Charlie.

Wonderful! said
the poetess from
East Coker.

Wonderful?
said Wendy:

I thought Bonnie
Prince Charlie
was something
of a wanker.

Lunch with Fleur

Somewhere in the freezer
Fleur had put a quiche.
She'd bought it for a street party
but it had rained and, in any case,
what a shame to give it up.

The quiche climbed into the freezer.
It sort of liked it: its parts becoming one,
a flying saucer, a frisbee, in Finchley.

It was a stroke of genius
to pull it out and watch it twitch
in the kitchen
rediscovering its pseudo-Gallic whatnot,
its thawing into chanson.
Quiche, you are my *chanson d'amour*:
small but perfect.

Have another piece, Fleur said
have another *chanson d'amour*.
Let's sing, I said, we could sing a duet.
I am tone deaf, I am a catastrophe
when it comes to duets
but there is something about the quiche
the O of oh and the O of oh
which makes me want to sing
and I want to dance the tango.

The quiche isn't a *chanson d'amour*
it's a tango by Astor Piazzolla
it's oblivion, it's total oblivion
it's the back streets of Buenos Aires
it's late afternoon, quiche, quiche are you ready?

Eternal Lunch

Curious how the middle classes never tire
of salmon. I've been sitting at the table
for fifty years – and the potatoes are lovely.
They're from the garden and the beans?
They're from the garden too. And the beetroot!
Yes mother, I have a distinct impression
the beetroot has risen up like a garrison
of legionnaires, from the garden, the lovely garden.

Everything's from the garden.
Fecundity! Fecundity! What?
Even Jenny, I believe, is from the garden.
I'd like to cover her with crème fraiche.
Is the salmon, I ask, also from the garden?
Of course not silly boy, the salmon is
                      from Scotland.

I can't breathe very well
and I'm clearing my throat
and now I'm saying it:
I'm saying, I've been sitting at the table
for fifty years and I'm wondering
if I might get down.

What on earth would you do once you were down?
my mother asks and my sister's saying
He'd run around the garden
and climb a tree and smoke a ciggy.
Yes, my mother says, and in any case
you can't get down until you've eaten
                      everything.

I've eaten rivers of salmon and fields of potato
and I've eaten so much beetroot
that I'm beginning to hallucinate.
I think dear mother I have eaten quite enough.

What about Jenny?
What about Jenny?
It's true of course
that nothing of Jenny
has passed my lips.

Oh Jenny of Woking give me your arm,
give me some homemade chutney
and a glass of ginger beer and I'll wash you down.

Dearest Jenny.

Tea with Brenda and Charles

A pair of buzzards wheeling over Ozleworth:
the Tomlinsons are taking tea on the lawn.
Holwell Farm is just a walk up the lane,
it belonged to Bruce and Elizabeth Chatwin.

Charles says, They make a sound before they swoop.
And Brenda says, Bruce wasn't listening.

Buddhism

After years of silence
my ex-wife sends me
a salami through the post.

I have to sign for it
and then I take it
into the flat and put it

in the fridge. And then I remember
a Calabrian neighbour
who hung his salamis

in every room in the house.
He was a doctor, or had at least
acquired some kind of

medical qualification –
but no luck finding a job.
He practised Buddhism

and this endowed him
with patience and good feelings
especially towards the salamis

which, it has to be said, gave
the apartment a particular aroma.
I like to keep my hand in,

he said. And he took out
a knife and began to chop the salami
in the hallway. I take my ex-wife's

salami out of the fridge and spend
much of the day looking at it.
Years of silence and then a salami!

And I look for a sharp knife
and slice off a piece which,
a little nervously, I eat. Delicious.

Supper in Lorsica

Fiona says, Shall we take these home?
I have to say I'm not exactly drooling.

She plucks them out of the earth
and walks towards the flames like Joan of Arc.

When we get back to the village
Signora Volpone leans out of the window:

Avete trovato i funghi?
Fiona holds up the yellowy things:

Careful, careful, says Signora Volpone,
they might be the eyes of the devil!

She sends down her son who is bare-chested
and good at everything.

He looks at the mushrooms and smells them
and then he waves his much-waved Italian finger.

Don't eat them, he says.
Thank God for that, I'm thinking.

And Fiona hurls them off the cliff.

Happy Carp Christmas

Prague

Usually you buy it
a couple of days
before Christmas
and throw it in the bath.
The children
give it a name
something like Marek the carp
and spend hours in the bathroom
falling head over heels
in love with it.
Then father kills it.

No one wants
to eat it,
especially the children.
It tastes of shit:
we call it the bottom eater.
No presents till
you've eaten your carp!

Everybody's shouting.
It's full of tiny bones
which get stuck
in the throat,
some people choke to death.

Happy Carp Christmas
to everyone!
Happy Crap Christmas
to everyone!

Bohemian Horseradish

For the first time in my life I pre-order
a taxi to pick me up at an airport.
I'm going to Prague. The taxi will cost 650 crowns.
I am almost certain that my internet exertions
will result in nothing. There is a reference number
which I remember to write on a slip of paper
and which I lose immediately. I'm rather
hoping there won't be anyone at the airport
holding up a piece of paper with my name on it.
I'm enjoying the idea of getting the wrong tram
and slipping into the obscure heart of nowhere.

So imagine my surprise when I walk out of
the airport and see among the throng
of names one which says MR STANDARD.
I am the visitor they anticipated; he will want
some Czech beer, a trip down the river
and some Roasted Pork Knee with a little
Bohemian Horseradish and he'll want to stand
on Charles Bridge with an arrow in his head.

A man with a scraggy beard and a beige jacket
and smelling of cigarettes clasps my hand –
Welcome to Prague Mr Standard, my name is Peter.
I will drive you to the Hotel Magnificent.

Smoking in my car is acceptable, he says
and throws out a butt-end with extravagance.
What do you do? he asks. I teach.
I had a Russian girlfriend with a diploma
in Shakespeare; no one could understand her,
not even Shakespeare! A joke, yes. I guess

she was very clever, I say. She was useless
at everything – a blonde with big boobs.
He take his hands off the steering wheel
to show how big they were. I bought her T-shirt
which said I AM A BLONDE – SORRY.
She went back to Moscow.

Bloody shit, he says, you talk so much I lose
the road, never mind I show you short cut –
He drives under a tunnel and then shoots
across a yap of land and re-joins the motorway.

Your English is very good, I say. Thank you.
I lived in Lewisham for two years.
I didn't need a diploma in Shakespeare!
Have another cigarette. Thank you.

The Hotel Magnificent is in a bad zone,
full of gypsies who will take your
money, your trousers and your nose –
I am thinking of Roasted English Nose
on a bed of Bohemian Horseradish.
And then as if he had a gift for discarding
last things he pulls off his nose, lowers
the window and throws it out. Double Portion
of Roasted Nose on a Bed of Bohemian . . .

I could take you to the Hotel Fantastic
where everything is top shit and you
could sleep in peace listening to Dvořák
of the trams with your nose in harmony.
Choice is despair, I say and in any case Peter
I booked a room at the Hotel Magnificent,
I'll take my chances. Oh Mr Standard, he says
(tapping his nose), I'm now wondering

if I haven't by mistake picked up the wrong man.
He leaves me at the Hotel Magnificent.
I pay him 650 crowns and he gives me a receipt.
He says, I like talking to you, my name is Peter.
If you want anything, this is my number:
blondes, diplomas, boys, drugs – my name is Peter.
I lived in Lewisham for two years.
I check in, lie on a bed and listen to the trams.

Next day I'm sitting in a scruffy park
full of dog shit and smoking a cigarette.
A young man – unmistakably a gypsy –
is pushing a baby towards me. I feel a twinge
at the end of my nose. When he gets to the bench
he stops and says something. I shrug.
The boy starts shouting and walks towards a bush
leaving the baby almost next to me.
When I look at the baby again it seems odd,
I'm wondering whether it's a stuffed baby.
It doesn't appear to have a nose.
The boy is having a slash in the bush,
it seems to be a very long slash and I notice
the park is full of gypsies with stuffed babies
(if, that is, they're stuffed). Oh Peter
I should have gone to the Hotel Fantastic,
even now I could be listening to Dvořák.
I can smell hot dogs from the hot dog stand.
How much longer will I be able to smell them?

Beata and Stephen

I'm lying in the dark.
I've been lying in the dark
for weeks. Occasionally
I get up and have a cigarette
and reach out for a painkiller.
Once there was a box of
sleeping pills but now the box
is empty. Right now
I would trade anything
for a Mogadon, so inert
so completely without small talk.

I stumble into the kitchen
imagining a plate of
grilled aubergines but what
I find is a wilderness.
The only good thing about
getting out of bed is that
you can find a way of getting
back . . . And then terrifyingly
the bell rings. Who on earth
would call now? My father
who is dead? My brother who is dead?
Is it my turn to have a ride
on the swing low sweet chariot?
I really ought to shave.
I open the door and discover
I have ordered a 12-inch
Domino pizza. Thank you, I say,
thank you so very much
for this 12-inch Domino pizza.

I don't eat much of the pizza
but it's good to know it's there
holding its own in a kitchen
beginning to look like Mogadishu.
I get back into bed and switch on
the radio. Everyone seems so happy
setting up businesses in China
or being terribly knowledgeable about
Antonia Fraser . . . Then suddenly
voices as intoxicating as a turtle dove.
Beata and Stephen, oh Beata and Stephen:
they would appear to be chatting
      on Radio Ether!

The Gargantuan Muffin Beauty Contest

We were at the Edison Hotel on West 47th Street
for the annual muffin beauty contest –
I can't tell you how pumped up we were.
Times Square was having another psychotic judder.
The bellhop was all thumbs up: Sir, have a nice day
and get one gratis. All those avenues of doors
and the Hispanic chambermaid who couldn't speak English.
Spider-Man was doing all that Spider-Man shit
just to get a bird's-eye view. Donna Summer
was almost dead and we were barely into spring.
I want to dance to Love to Love You Baby, I want to groan.
I've never seen so many high quality muffins.
If I wasn't a religious man, and maybe I wasn't
I would have said the muffins were walking on water:
I've never felt so half and half. Have you read the Bible?
The bellhop said: You ain't seen muffin yet.
They were drifting in from Queens, Brooklyn, Harlem,
the Bronx, Manhattan muffins too and that weird
cute Coke-faced muffin who'd taken the subway
from Coney Island. If only I were a betting man,
but hey I am a betting man, it's Coney Island every time.
Lou Reed isn't getting any younger. Zappa said
Girl you thought he was a man but he was a muffin,
he hung around till you found he didn't know nuthin.
In the lobby Nina Simone was singing, I loves you Muffin
and in the restroom they piped in Mack the Knife:
Hey Sookie Taudry, Jenny Diver, Polly Peachum
and old Miss Lulu Brown. *Muffin The Romance*
was the biggest show in town. We were hurtling back
to the 1970s and sometimes the 1970s are almost
as good as the 1930s. I want my muffins to be ahistorical:

shit just to say *ahistorical* makes me joyful.
I saw Leonard Cohen crooning with a couple
of octogenarian muffins and I'm telling you now
the lobby was pleasantly disturbing. You may find
yourself behind the wheel of a large automobile.
You may find yourself in another part of the world.
You may find yourself at the gargantuan muffin beauty contest
and you may ask yourself, Well, how did I get here?
Times Square was having another psychotic judder.
Love is in the air, it's in the whisper of the trees.
This is not America, this is the cover version:
sun, sex, sin, divine intervention, death and destruction,
welcome to *The Sodom and Gomorrah Show*.
All those white muffins trying to be black muffins!
Give us our daily muffin, save us from temptation.
Jimmy Buffet was singing, Why don't we get drunk
and screw? In Times Square the most beautiful muffins
in the world were hanging on a thousand screens.
Where are my singing Tibetan balls? Am I dead?

Donut

O Benjamin P. Lovell, 19,
from Oneanta, New York State
who appears in the Police Blotter
in Thursday's *Daily Star* for
unlawful possession of marijuana.
The Police Blotter hangs just
below the cast of *Hairpsray*
rehearsing at the SUNY ONEANTA
GOODRICH THEATER
where the girl playing Tracy
Turnblad looks as if she's been
helping herself to donuts:
maybe the donuts we were eating
at Barlow's General Stores, Treadwell.
Do you ever get an upstate rush?
I've never been crazy about donuts
but these are the aristocrats
of the donut world and I salute them.

And I hope, Benjamin, your mom
isn't going to be too mad as she casts
her eye down the Police Blotter
and sees your name there, *You little shit!*
And I hope the authorities remember
being young when the whole world
sometimes seemed somehow like
a gargantuan donut that either pulled
you to its bosom (Oh Tracy!) or kicked
down – somewhere – to the bloodstream.
Sweet donut, do I love thee? I haven't
mentioned Brando K. Goodluck, 18,

from Manhattan, charged with seventh-degree
criminal possession of a controlled
substance. O Brando, O Brando
what were you thinking?

As I put a donut in my mouth
I'm thinking I wouldn't mind
a joint, and in any case maybe
these donuts are a little dangerous
and I wonder what would happen
if the rules got jumbled up
and the girl playing Tracy Turnblad
slid down the page
and found herself in the Police Blotter
charged with unlawful possession
of a donut. Suddenly America feels
different and I like it.
Police Blotters throughout the nation
packed with donut-heads and half the country
on the run as college girls make
secret calls and meet their dealers
in dusty ghost towns, sweet
vapours drifting through the trees.

Oh America, where even the robins
are bigger, where every car that
slides into the forecourt of Barlow
General Stores is a Dodge, where
half the population is chasing
the perfect donut. Let's imagine
that Benjamin P. Lovell and
Brando K. Goodluck, nice slim boys
who've never touched a donut
in their lives, wander into Barlow's

and roll a joint and talk about those
losers who kneel down before 'the big one'.
They know the girl who was playing
Tracy Turnblad. She was sweet, they say,
who went and threw it all away
for a sleazy bun with a hole in it.
They pass the joint to me and I can
feel the donuts I stuffed in haste
somewhere down my slacks. I blush.
Real shame, I say. Mrs Barlow says
You boys want more coffee?
The donuts on her shelves have gone.

Dinner with Val

Val was saying, I just got messages through
and put them in a box and at the end of the war
they gave me a medal. No idea what happened to it.
And when the pilots were floating in the sky
it was exhilarating and we raced across the fields
hoping the men would be okay and hoping
for a bit of parachute. Some of the Germans
were charming, such a shame they were German.

Parachute pants were the thing and Veronica
actually got married in a parachute, mind you
she was marrying a pilot – a lovely man –
even though he had lost a leg which,
I suppose, made some things awkward.
And then I worked in the War Office pushing
planes and ships around with a stick and
on one occasion Winston came in with a dog.

It was a black dog, and if I'm not mistaken
it had a funny eye – oh dear should I have said that?
Winston said, Do carry on and goodness how we did.
I saw a ship lurking around off Scotland and
shoved it into the Pacific – that whizzed things up.

I got another medal for that.

The Recipe

for Toby

All I could remember
about the recipe was
that you had to separate
the eggs, as if the eggs
had a pathological dislike
for each other, or maybe,
like teenage kids, they just
egged each other on,
or maybe they were bad:
I put one in the pantry
and the other in the small
room along the corridor
and I said to myself,
not without a feeling of
triumph: I have separated
    the eggs.

EAST FINCHLEY